FIND YOUR
ADVENTURE

A JOURNAL
>>— FOR EXPLORING —<<
HOME & AWAY

— *by* —

NICOLE LARUE

CHANGE THE WAY
YOU EXPECT THE WORLD TO BE.

THIS

Adventure

>— BELONGS TO —<

_____

Esteemed ADVENTURERS,

SAY HELLO TO AN EXTRAORDINARY,
UNCONVENTIONAL & UTTERLY MEANINGFUL
WAY TO NAVIGATE YOUR WORLD.

WHETHER YOU PLAN TO GO NEAR OR FAR,
HERE TO THERE, OR HITHER & YON, YOU CAN MAKE
EVEN THE MOST FAMILIAR, GENERALLY HUMDRUM,
OR DECIDEDLY ORDINARY PLACES YOU GO
QUITE EXCEPTIONAL.

Don't delay! MERELY OPEN THE BOOK AND STEP OUT
YOUR FRONT DOOR. **GET GOING IN ANY ORDER.**
Skip pages. **PICK SOMETHING THAT FITS YOUR MOOD**
OR STRIKES YOUR FANCY. ADJUST YOUR JOURNEY IN
THE MIDDLE. **THERE'S NO 'RIGHT' WAY** TO USE THIS
LITTLE BOOK SO TAKE YOUR UNBRIDLED BRAVERY &
WEND YOUR WAY THROUGH THE WORLD. REPORT ALL
YOUR FINDINGS, JOT DOWN YOUR EVERY MUSING,
CAPTURE YOUR VARIOUS INKLINGS
& CORRAL YOUR NOTIONS ONE BY ONE.

Sally forth, YOU PROMISING WANDERER,
YOU FACT-HUNGRY ANTHROPOLOGIST, YOU MAGNANIMOUS
JOURNEYER, YOU EVER-INTREPID EXPLORER—
YOU ADVENTURER!

>>— *Now,* LET'S BEGIN. —<<

TAKE THIS
BOOK

(CIRCLE ALL THAT APPLY)

ANYWHERE • EVERYWHERE • SOMEWHERE

NOWHERE • ELSEWHERE • OTHERWHERE

OUT AND ABOUT • HITHER AND YON

FORTH AND BACK • HERE TO THERE

THIS PLACE • THAT PLACE • SOMEPLACE

ANY OLD PLACE • TO PARTS UNKNOWN

HIGH AND LOW • NEAR AND FAR • FAR AND WIDE

OUT OF THE WAY • EVERY WHICH WAY

ON A ROADTRIP • TO A PARK • THROUGH A CITY

TO THE COUNTRY • OUT TO SEA • ON A TRAIN

OFF THE BEATEN PATH

ALONG
-WITH THESE-
UN-RULES,
MERE GUIDELINES & LIGHT ETIQUETTE,
MIGHT THIS JOURNAL IMPLORE YOU TO:

....

TAKE THE SCENIC ROUTE · DILLY-DALLY

LOOK PEOPLE IN THE EYE · THANK EVERYONE

TEETER INTO THE UNKNOWN · BE OPEN

QUESTION EVERYTHING · SMILE AT STRANGERS

DRINK PLENTY OF WATER · TRY NEW THINGS

DEFY THE LAWS OF GRAVITY · TAKE CHANCES

BREAK THE RULES · DON'T THINK TOO MUCH

TRUST YOUR INSTINCTS · LISTEN WITH INTEREST

DANCE FREELY · BE OTHERWORLDLY

LEAVE YOUR WATCH AT HOME

TAKE NOTHING FOR GRANTED · HEM & HAW

DRESS ACCORDINGLY · LIVE ADVENTUROUSLY

ALTER YOUR JOURNEY AND BE

Awesome.

- Adventurer -
PROFILE

FULL NAME:

NICKNAME:

PEN NAME:

Date of Birth:

Your Sign:

Your Height:

Eye Color:

OCCUPATION (OR DREAM JOB)

3

PET PEEVES:

Major Allergies:

Activity Level:

1   2   3   4   5   6   7   8   9   10
(sloth)   (hummingbird)

Undisputed PHOBIAS:

_____   _____
_____   _____
_____   _____
_____   _____
_____   _____

Emergency Contact:

TELEPHONE NUMBER:

★ (FOR RARE CASES OF FOOD POISONING, ONE TOO MANY BUG BITES, OR THE OCCASIONAL MIX-UP)

WHERE TO NEXT:

_____   _____
_____   _____
_____   _____
_____   _____
_____   _____

OTHER NOTES:

_____
_____

MAYBE YOU HAVE AN OVERLOADED PURSE OR A SIMPLE BACKPACK OR EVEN A TRICKED-OUT TOTE? HOWEVER YOU HAUL, YOU'RE SURE TO HAVE A HANDFUL OF ITEMS YOU CAN'T LIVE WITHOUT. A FAVORED NOTEBOOK BY CHANCE? MINTY GUM IN CASE OF A NERVOUS SOCIAL ENCOUNTER? A SNACK FOR THE RARE CHANCE YOU ARE SO BUSY ADVENTURING AND MISS LUNCH?

....

Draw and label the essential items you are carrying,

YOU TEND TO CARRY, YOU OUGHT TO CARRY:

HAVE YOU *Ever*

- ○ Distributed secret messages
- ○ Taken a train
- ○ Eaten an insect
- ○ Talked to a stranger
- ○ Tried bubble tea
- ○ Cooked foreign cuisine
- ○ Swapped identities
- ○ Visited a nude beach
- ○ Played a superhero
- ○ Eaten a dumpling
- ○ Worn a clown nose through town
- ○ Gone skydiving
- ○ Talked in pig latin
- ○ Revealed a secret
- ○ Used chopsticks
- ○ Fed wildlife
- ○ Had a pen pal
- ○ Taken a taxi
- ○ Been seasick

- ○ Carried around a magic wand
- ○ Paid for someone else's meal
- ○ Spent a day in silence
- ○ Held an alligator
- ○ Eaten a progressive dinner
- ○ Ridden a double-decker bus
- ○ Met a famous person
- ○ Taken a stranger to lunch
- ○ Eaten breakfast for dinner
- ○ Done extensive people watching
- ○ Said yes to everything
- ○ Taken pictures in the dark
- ○ Attended a tea ceremony
- ○ Walked through an outdoor market
- ○ Eaten with your hands
- ○ Walked around in a cape
- ○ Gone on a bus, train, bicycle & plane in a single day

Give yourself points if you want to: _____

MY DREAM
Adventures LIST

WRITE DOWN THE EPIC ADVENTURES YOU PLAN ON TAKING IN YOUR LIFETIME.
SKY'S THE LIMIT! UNLESS YOU DREAM OF OUTER SPACE, THAT IS ...

OH, ALL THE
Little places I'LL GO!

NOW THAT WE'VE COVERED THE BIG DREAMS, WHERE ELSE DO YOU WANT TO VACATION, VISIT, OR OTHERWISE CALL UPON? DEFINITELY A HERE, A THERE, AND EVERYWHERE IN BETWEEN KIND OF LIST!

Maybe,
**JUST MAYBE,
SOME OF THESE
MAKE THE LIST?**

THAT OVERLY
EXPENSIVE
RESTAURANT

THE NEW HIP
COFFEE SHOP

THE TOP OF
THAT BEAUTIFUL
MOUNTAIN

ALL THE STOPS
ALONG YOUR
TRAIN LINE

THAT BEACH
YOU'VE HAD YOUR
EYE ON

THAT TRAIL NEAR
YOUR HOUSE

THAT FOREST
YOU'VE YET TO
DISCOVER

And on and on
AND ON AND ON!

SOMEDAY

I *am* GOING TO...

CREATE A NOTEWORTHY LIST OF LIFE-SIZE AMBITIONS, LOFTY DREAMS &
BIG PLANS. THIS IS A BONA FIDE TO-DO LIST, SO BE GENUINELY FEARLESS,
THOUGHTFULLY FIERCE & TRUE TO YOURSELF. ADD START DATES TO ALL
THAT'S ON YOUR LIST!

MY
Adventure
MANIFESTO

I, _____ (NAME, NICKNAME, PEN NAME),

HEREBY HOLD THESE _____ (S) TO BE

UNQUESTIONABLE (UNLESS I CHANGE MY MIND).

THIS IS MY _____ .

THE WORLD AWAITS AND I SHALL _____ .

THESE UNSCRIPTED STORIES ARE _____ .

I AVOID NOTHING AND I WILL NOT _____ .

I _____ BY MY OWN RULES. I REGARD ADVENTURING

AS MY ONE, SOLE _____ . I WILL SHINE _____ .

I WILL LAUGH AT MYSELF AND _____ WITH ABANDON.

I WILL ABSORB _____ , ENJOY _____ ,

BREATHE _____ , AND TARRY _____ .

I AM SOLELY RESPONSIBLE FOR CULTIVATING

_____ AND CELEBRATING _____ .

I WILL USE MY HANDS, AND _____ MY STORY

AND BE AUTHENTICALLY _____ . I WILL

_____ AWESOMENESS AND SOLVE GREAT _____ (S).

I PLAN TO BE THE HERO OF MY OWN _____ AND AN

ADVENTURER OF _____ AND CANNOT BE STOPPED.

IT'S ME _____ THE WORLD. *So away we go!*

A

Chapter of

WANDERING

ADVENTURES

WANDERING

ADVENTURES

This CHAPTER IS FOR EVERY BRAND

OF VOYAGER, ANY PROMISING WANDERER,

AND ALL THE DELIGHTFUL MEANDERERS.

TAKE YOUR BOOK AND VEER OFF,

BREAK LOOSE, MOVE AS MUCH AS YOU

CAN MUSTER, SURRENDER TO YOUR

RESTLESSNESS, TRAVEL ABOUT, BE OPEN

TO DISCOVERIES, GO PLACES, GO ASTRAY,

GET LOST FOR A TIME (THOUGH, PLEASE DO

FIND YOUR WAY BACK), CHOOSE ANY WHICH WAY

& BE A WILLING WANDERER FOR A DAY.

ALL RIGHT THEN, *run along!*

ON **THE** Road

CREATE A SERIES OF DELIGHTFUL TRANSPORTATION ART! DRAW AND DOODLE WHILE RIDING THE BUS, THE TRAIN, OR ON AN AIRPLANE, AS A PASSENGER IN A CAR, TAXI, OR TUK-TUK, WHILE MEANDERING DOWN A TRAIL, ALONG A SIDEWALK, OR ACROSS A SANDY BEACH.

Date:
....

DRAWN WHILE:

....
....

Date:
....

DRAWN WHILE:

....
....

Date:
....

DRAWN WHILE:

....
....

Date:
....

DRAWN WHILE:

....
....

Date:
....

DRAWN WHILE:

....
....

Date:
....

DRAWN WHILE:

....
....

Date:
....

DRAWN WHILE:

....
....

Date:
....

DRAWN WHILE:

....
....

Friend
ADVENTURE

....

TODAY, SKIP THE RESTAURANTS. PACK UP ALL

THE GOOD-TASTING TIDBITS YOU CAN FIND,

GRAB YOUR BEST CHUM, YOUR WILD ROOMMATE,

YOUR PARTNER IN CRIME, OR YOUR CLOSEST PAL,

AND SHARE A PICNIC OUTSIDE! WHERE DID YOU

GO? DID YOU DEVISE A PLAN? DID YOU WANDER

FAR? HOW DID YOU DECIDE? WHO DID YOU

SHARE IT WITH? DESCRIBE YOUR SURROUNDINGS.

_____

_____

_____

_____

_____

_____

_____

_____

_____

_____

_____

_____

Picnic Location: .... *Date:* ....

Draw

MEANDERING

DETAILS

SOMETHING NEAR

Date: /   Location:

SOMETHING FAR

Date: / Location:

SOMETHING WILD

Date: / Location:

SOMETHING IN PLAIN SIGHT

Date: / Location:

SOMETHING YOU HAD TO CLIMB TO SEE

Date: / Location:

SOMETHING ON YOUR PATH

Date: ⎰ Location:

SOMETHING CURIOUS

Date: ⎰ Location:

SOMETHING GRAZING

Date: Location:

SOMETHING LOST

Date: Location:

PHOTO *Adventure*

EMBARK ON A PHOTO SCAVENGER HUNT!

....

TAKE PICTURES AND RECORD YOUR FINDINGS WITH DATES
& LOCATIONS FOR A REALLY COOL FUTURE ALBUM!

☐ **YOUR SHOES**
DATE: LOCATION:

Description
_____
_____

☐ **A MODE OF TRANSPORTATION**
DATE: LOCATION:

Description
_____
_____

☐ **A PATH**
DATE: LOCATION:

Description
_____
_____

☐ **A BUSY THOROUGHFARE**
DATE: LOCATION:

Description
_____
_____

☐ **A WHEEL**
DATE: LOCATION:

Description
_____
_____

☐ **THE LONG WAY AROUND**
DATE: LOCATION:

Description
_____
_____

☐ **AN ALLEY**
DATE: LOCATION:

Description
_____
_____

☐ **A PASSAGEWAY**
DATE: LOCATION:

Description
_____
_____

☐ **A FOOTPATH**
DATE: LOCATION:

Description
_____
_____

☐ **A SOLITARY BIT OF NATURE**
DATE: LOCATION:

Description
_____
_____

☐ **SOMETHING COMMON**
DATE: LOCATION:

Description
_____
_____

☐ **DOWNTOWN**
DATE: LOCATION:

Description
_____
_____

☐ **SOMETHING FLYING**
DATE: LOCATION:

Description
_____
_____

☐ **SOMETHING NUMBERED**
DATE: LOCATION:

Description
_____
_____

☐ **AN ODD DOOR**
DATE: LOCATION:

Description
_____
_____

☐ **AN OPEN WINDOW**
DATE: LOCATION:

Description
_____
_____

☐ **A SHORTCUT**
DATE: LOCATION:

Description
_____
_____

☐ **A TINY TRAIL**
DATE: LOCATION:

Description
_____
_____

☐ **AN ENTRANCE**
DATE: LOCATION:

Description
_____
_____

☐ **AN EXIT**
DATE: LOCATION:

Description
_____
_____

☐ **OTHER**
DATE: LOCATION:

Description
_____
_____

☐ **OTHER**
DATE: LOCATION:

Description
_____
_____

A MOVEABLE *Feast*

HAVE A PROGRESSIVE DINNER, A SAFARI SUPPER,
A FOOD TOUR, OR A MOVING BANQUET!

....

MIX WITH DIFFERENT LOCATIONS & GO TO
A DIFFERENT PLACE FOR EACH COURSE:

FANCY HORS D'OEUVRES:

TASTY SOUPS AND SALADS:

A LAVISH MAIN COURSE:

A MODEST PALATE CLEANSER:

A DELECTABLE DESSERT:

AFTER-DINNER DRINKS:

RECORD & RATE EVERYTHING YOU EAT & DRINK!

Date: ....

Chart **YOUR** COURSE

TODAY, SWITCH THINGS UP AND TAKE A DETOUR – FIND SOMETHING OFF THE BEATEN PATH
OR REVERSE A PLANNED ITINERARY! MAP YOUR NEWLY TAKEN COURSE RIGHT HERE
ON YOUR PAGE! ADD THE INTERESTING DISCOVERIES YOU ENCOUNTER ALONG THE WAY!

Date: _____

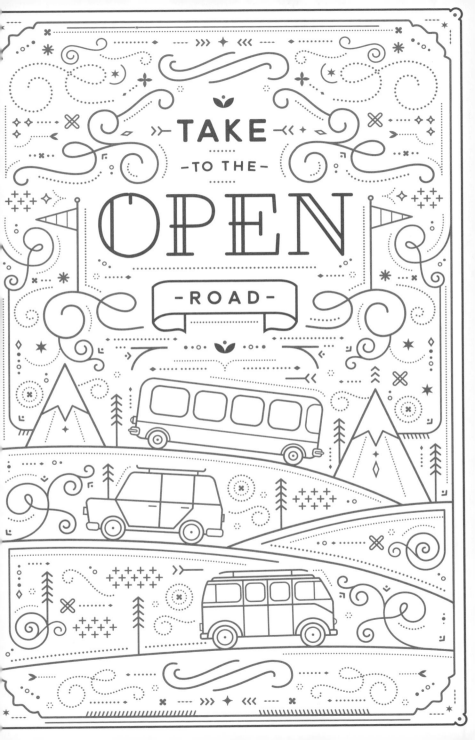

25 THINGS I'VE DISCOVERED
WHILE *Wandering*:

1. _____

2. _____

3. _____

4. _____

5. _____

6. _____

7. _____

8. _____

9. _____

10. _____

11. _____

12. _____

13. _____

14.

15.

16.

17.

18.

19.

20.

21.

22.

23.

24.

25.

WANDER

id="2" /> *Just* CHECK ALL THAT APPLY.

- ○ BECAUSE ALL GOOD PIONEERS WANDER
- ○ TO SEEK MAGIC EVERY DAY
- ○ TO NUDGE MY COMFORT ZONE
- ○ AS A MOVE OF LIBERATION
- ○ TO BE SLIGHTLY GUTSY
- ○ TO EXPLORE, YET, SOME MORE
- ○ FOR DEEP, PHILOSOPHICAL PURPOSES
- ○ TO LEAVE NO STONE UNTURNED
- ○ TO DELIGHT IN THE MEANDERING
- ○ TO BE AN AUDACIOUS SEEKER
- ○ TO FIND MY WILD SIDE
- ○ TO SEE, TO SEE & TO SEE!
- ○ AS A WAY OF PUSHING MY OWN LIMITS
- ○ JUST TO BREAK LOOSE
- ○ AS A WAY TO MAKE WILD DISCOVERIES
- ○ TO PICK UP MY FEET
- ○ TO FIND A NEW PATH
- ○ TO GO WHERE THE WIND BLOWS ME
- ○ TO BE AS UNTAMED AS THE OCEAN
- ○ SO I'LL NEVER LOSE MY FIRE
- ○ TO BE BRAVE WITH MY LIFE
- ○ SO I DON'T TAKE ANYTHING FOR GRANTED
- ○ SO THAT I MIGHT DANCE WITH ABANDON
- ○ IT'S A FINE DAY TO BE A WANDERER
- ○ TO BE AN EXPLORER OF THE WORLD
- ○ TO LIVE FREE
- ○ _____
- ○ _____
- ○ _____

Date: _____

AN UNEXPECTED TURN

TODAY, GET LOST ON PURPOSE! SEEK SOMETHING UNFAMILIAR, TAKE A CHANCE, SCOUT OUT A DIFFERENT APPROACH & EXPLORE OTHER PATHWAYS, THOROUGHFARES, HIGHWAYS & BYWAYS! KEEP TRACK OF THE NEW THINGS YOU FIND!

....

....

....

....

....

....

....

....

....

....

....

....

....

....

....

....

....

....

....

....

....

....

Try
THIS:

TAKE YOUR
SECOND RIGHT,
YOUR FIRST
TWO LEFTS, AND
THEN ADD IN
ANOTHER RIGHT
AT THE END,
FOR GOOD MEASURE.

LEAVE YOUR MAP
AT HOME AND
HEAD OUT!

YOU DON'T ALWAYS
HAVE TO KNOW
WHERE YOU'RE
GOING!

Date: _____

ON *Foot*

**TODAY, WALK EVERYWHERE. PICK UP YOUR FEET, PERAMBULATE, HOOF IT,
SAUNTER ALONG & SEE WHERE THOSE LEGS CAN TAKE YOU — ACROSS
UNEVEN SIDEWALKS, COBBLESTONE ALLEYWAYS, SMOOTHLY PAVED
STREETS, RUGGED RAILWAYS & MUDDY TRAILS.**

RECREATE THE TEXTURES YOU COME UPON IN YOUR BOOK AS YOU CARRY YOURSELF ABOUT.

PLACE:

_____

PATHWAY TYPE:
TIME:

PLACE:

_____

PATHWAY TYPE:
TIME:

PLACE:

_____

PATHWAY TYPE:
TIME:

PLACE:

_____

PATHWAY TYPE:
TIME:

PLACE:

_____

PATHWAY TYPE:
TIME:

PLACE:

_____

PATHWAY TYPE:
TIME:

HOP, SKIP &
JUMP

TODAY, CHANGE YOUR MODE OF TRANSPORTATION
(or, umm, sort of). SKIP FROM PLACE TO PLACE, *yeah, just skip.*
FROM DOOR TO DOOR AND FROM HERE TO THERE. SKIP SUBTLY
OR CAUTIOUSLY OR OUTRAGEOUSLY. BUT, SKIP. SEE WHAT HAPPENS
& RECORD THE REACTIONS!

Date: _____

Passing NOTES

·····························

TODAY, SPREAD KINDNESS. TAKE A SHEET OF PAPER
& CUT, TEAR, SHAPE, TRIM, OR OTHERWISE
DIVIDE IT INTO SMALL NOTE-SIZE BITS. WRITE
GRACIOUS, FRIENDLY, GOOD-HEARTED THOUGHTS ON
EACH SMALL SCRAP. AS YOU MEANDER THROUGH
YOUR DAY, SECRETLY SLIP, RANDOMLY PLACE
& SNEAKINGLY LEAVE ALL YOUR HAPPY
NOTES FOR OTHERS TO FIND.

(Record your secret notes in this book.)

_____

_____

_____

_____

_____

_____

_____

_____

_____

_____

Date : ....

Spick **AND** SPAN

BE AN UNOFFICIAL CITY, URBAN, OR NEIGHBORHOOD VOLUNTEER FOR THE DAY.
TAKE TO THE ROAD & TIDY UP, MAKE IT ALL SPARKLINGLY CLEAN & NEAT
AS A BUTTON! DRAW ALL THAT YOU MANAGED TO THROW AWAY.

Date: _____ Location: _____

FREE
WHEELING

Get out the bikes! PULL OUT YOUR OWN SET OF WHEELS,
VISIT A LOCAL BIKE RENTAL SHOP, OR BORROW ONE FROM A FRIEND
& CYCLE EVERYWHERE. WHAT NEW THINGS DID YOU NOTICE,
FIND, HAPPEN UPON, COME ACROSS, BUMP INTO, OR NOT ANTICIPATE?

DATE .... WEATHER ....

BICYCLE TYPE .... BICYCLE COLOR ....

Around TOWN

Today, MAKE UP YOUR OWN WALKING TOUR. MOST PLACES HAVE A SECTION OF TOWN THAT THEY SHOWCASE FOR VISITORS, GUESTS & NEWCOMERS. CREATE A MAP OF YOUR FAVORITES, YOUR TOP CHOICES & YOUR BEST DISCOVERIES, THEN LIST THE LOCATIONS ON YOUR MAP. THERE'S PROBABLY MORE OUT THERE THAN MEETS THE EYE!

Date: _____

MY COLLECTION

OVER THE COURSE OF A WEEK, SET A GOAL TO COLLECT, AMASS, STOCKPILE, HEAP,
OR HOARD ALL THINGS THAT MAKE YOU FEEL LIKE AN EXPERIENCED WANDERER!
(MAYBE A COMPASS, A WELL-WORN PAIR OF SHOES, YOUR NEW ROCK COLLECTION, OR
A PILE OF TRAVEL NOTES.) DRAW, IDENTIFY, OR RECORD THEM HERE.

ITEM ....
Date:
....

ITEM ....
Date:
....

ITEM ....
Date:
....

ITEM ....
Date:
....

ITEM ....
Date:
....

ITEM ....
Date:
....

ITEM ....
Date:
....

ITEM ....
Date:
....

RESTLESS

THINGS TO *Remember:*

Chapter
TWO

A

Chapter of

NOTEWORTHY

ADVENTURES

NOTEWORTHY

ADVENTURES

This CHAPTER WILL IMPLORE YOU TO BE
A RELENTLESS DETECTIVE, A FACT-HUNGRY
ANTHROPOLOGIST & A PERPETUAL SCOUT.
SO GRAB YOUR BOOK, ZERO IN ON YOUR
SURROUNDINGS, INVESTIGATE EVERY ANGLE,
TAKE A GOOD LOOK, LOOK AGAIN, PORE OVER
& PROBE INTO, BE CEASELESSLY LOOKING,
CONCENTRATE UPON THE DETAILS, ENDEAVOR
TO EXAMINE THE MINUTIAE, SIFT THROUGH
THE MUNDANE, MAGNIFY YOUR FINDINGS,
EXPLORE THE FAMILIAR & CELEBRATE
EVERY LITTLE DETAILED HAPPENING.
NOW, *follow your nose!*

ADVENTURE

·······························

TOTE AROUND

·······························

WHAT'S IN YOUR BAG? DRAW
EVERY ITEM YOU'RE CURRENTLY
CARRYING WITH YOU & LET THE
CONTENTS BE YOUR GUIDE!
WHAT'S THE MOST VALUABLE
ITEM YOU PACKED (REMEMBERING
VALUE RARELY SUGGESTS
MONEY)? WHAT SHOULD YOU
HAVE LEFT BEHIND? UH, OH!
WHAT DID YOU FORGET?

ITEM NO. ··············
Date:

ITEM NO. ··············
Date:

ITEM NO. ··············
Date:

ITEM NO. ··············
Date:

ITEM NO. ··············
Date:

ITEM NO. ··············
Date:

ITEM NO. ....
Date:

ITEM NO. ....
Date:

ITEM NO. ....
Date:

ITEM NO. ....
Date:

ITEM NO. ....
Date:

ITEM NO. ....
Date:

ITEM NO. ....
Date:

ITEM NO. ....
Date:

PHOTOGENIC *Foods*

CREATE A FOOD-SELFIES GALLERY!

CAPTURE AND CHRONICLE UNEXPECTED TREATS, MORSELS, NIBBLES &
BITES YOU SAMPLE. TAKE PHOTOS & NOTES OF EVERY ADVENTUROUS BITE.

FOOD:

DATE: LOCATION:

◯ I COULD EAT THIS EVERY DAY!
◯ IT'S AN ACQUIRED TASTE.
◯ NEVER AGAIN!

FOOD:

DATE: LOCATION:

◯ I COULD EAT THIS EVERY DAY!
◯ IT'S AN ACQUIRED TASTE.
◯ NEVER AGAIN!

FOOD:

DATE: LOCATION:

◯ I COULD EAT THIS EVERY DAY!
◯ IT'S AN ACQUIRED TASTE.
◯ NEVER AGAIN!

FOOD:

DATE: LOCATION:

◯ I COULD EAT THIS EVERY DAY!
◯ IT'S AN ACQUIRED TASTE.
◯ NEVER AGAIN!

FOOD:

DATE: LOCATION:

◯ I COULD EAT THIS EVERY DAY!
◯ IT'S AN ACQUIRED TASTE.
◯ NEVER AGAIN!

FOOD:

DATE: LOCATION:

◯ I COULD EAT THIS EVERY DAY!
◯ IT'S AN ACQUIRED TASTE.
◯ NEVER AGAIN!

FOOD:

DATE: LOCATION:

◯ I COULD EAT THIS EVERY DAY!
◯ IT'S AN ACQUIRED TASTE.
◯ NEVER AGAIN!

FOOD:

DATE: LOCATION:

◯ I COULD EAT THIS EVERY DAY!
◯ IT'S AN ACQUIRED TASTE.
◯ NEVER AGAIN!

Mirror IMAGE

LOOK FOR UNEXPECTED PLACES, LOCATIONS & SITUATIONS WHERE YOU CAN PHOTOGRAPH YOUR REFLECTION. SPOT EVERY CHANCE PLACE YOU CAN! NOTICE STORE WINDOWS, SHALLOW PONDS, DARK SUNGLASSES, SHINY SIDING, BODIES OF WATER, BITS OF CHROME, TRAFFIC MIRRORS, POLISHED METAL & WHATEVER ELSE YOU HAPPEN UPON. FIND WAYS TO BE INNOVATIVE & BE PERPETUALLY LOOKING!

Date:

Location:

Details:

Date:

Location:

Details:

Date:

Location:

Details:

Date:

Location:

Details:

Date:

Location:

Details:

Date:

Location:

Details:

PHOTO *Adventure*

EMBARK ON A PHOTO SCAVENGER HUNT!

....

RECORD YOUR FINDINGS WITH DATES & LOCATIONS
FOR A REALLY COOL FUTURE ALBUM!

☐ INTERESTING PATTERNS

DATE: LOCATION:

Description

_____

_____

☐ A MISSPELLED WORD

DATE: LOCATION:

Description

_____

_____

☐ AN ANIMAL CLOUD SHAPE

DATE: LOCATION:

Description

_____

_____

☐ A SPECK

DATE: LOCATION:

Description

_____

_____

☐ SOMETHING SEE-THROUGH

DATE: LOCATION:

Description

_____

_____

☐ SOMETHING ERASED

DATE: LOCATION:

Description

_____

_____

☐ A FLOURISH

DATE: LOCATION:

Description

_____

_____

☐ A FADING COLOR

DATE: LOCATION:

Description

_____

_____

☐ AN INCH OF SOMETHING

DATE: LOCATION:

Description

_____

_____

☐ AN UNEXPECTED CLUE

DATE: LOCATION:

Description

_____

_____

Friend
ADVENTURE

....

ASK A FRIEND, PARTNER, OR NEW PAL TO SHARE
A DETECTIVE'S ADVENTURE WITH YOU BY CREATING
A SCAVENGER HUNT FOR TWO! COME UP WITH
A LIST TOGETHER & FOLLOW THE TWISTS,
TURNS & PECULIAR PATHWAYS THROUGH THE
NEIGHBORHOOD STREETS & SLEUTH OUT EACH
ITEM ON YOUR LIST. READY, SET, GO!

Things to find:

_____

_____

_____

_____

_____

_____

_____

_____

_____

_____

_____

Where you found them:

_____

_____

_____

_____

_____

_____

_____

_____

_____

_____

_____

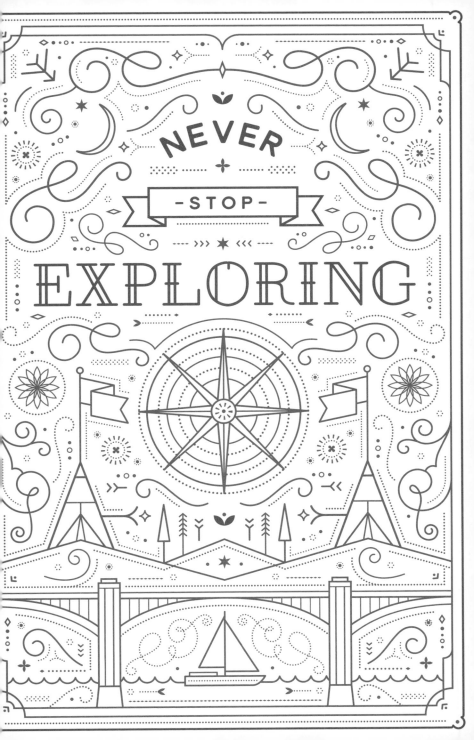

25 THINGS I'VE DISCOVERED
WHILE *Exploring:*

1. _____

2. _____

3. _____

4. _____

5. _____

6. _____

7. _____

8. _____

9. _____

10. _____

11. _____

12. _____

13. _____

14.

15.

16.

17.

18.

19.

20.

21.

22.

23.

24.

25.

why

I MUST

INVESTIGATE

Just
CHECK
ALL
THAT
APPLY

- ○ BECAUSE THAT'S WHAT ALL GOOD EXPLORERS DO
- ○ IN ORDER TO STAY WHOLLY INQUISITIVE
- ○ BECAUSE ADVENTURE AWAITS
- ○ TO SEARCH FOR THE UNDISCOVERED
- ○ FOR INQUIRING INTO THE UNEXPLORED
- ○ BECAUSE I'M A SCOUT
- ○ IN ORDER TO UNDERSTAND THE WORLD
- ○ IT'S A FINE DAY TO RECONNOITER
- ○ BECAUSE I WANT TO LEAVE A DETAILED ACCOUNT
- ○ TO SEEK NEW ADVENTURES
- ○ TO LEAVE NO STONE UNTURNED
- ○ BECAUSE I HAVE A PLAN
- ○ TO TURN EVERYTHING INSIDE OUT
- ○ BECAUSE IT'S MY ADVENTURE
- ○ TO FOLLOW A MAP TO ITS EDGES
- ○ TO QUESTION EVERYTHING
- ○ BECAUSE I'M A FULL-TIME TRAILBLAZER
- ○ BECAUSE I MUST PUT EVERYTHING TO THE TEST
- ○ OUT OF SHEER, EAGER CURIOSITY
- ○ TO HAVE A GOOD, LONG LOOK-SEE
- ○ TO TAP INTO MY INNER SPY
- ○ TO TRAVERSE MORE THAN I EVER HAVE
- ○ AS A WAY OF EXAMINING THE UNEXAMINED
- ○ BECAUSE THE DESTINATION IS VAGUE
- ○ TO TAKE A GOOD LOOK
- ○ BECAUSE I'M AN INVESTIGATOR AT HEART
- ○ _____
- ○ _____
- ○ _____

Date: _____

WHAT'S IN A
NAME?

LIST ALL OF THE STREET NAMES YOU ENCOUNTER.
WRITE A POEM USING AS MANY AS YOU CAN & MAIL IT TO A FRIEND!

(Come on, you've done stranger things!)

ALL **IN THE** *Details*

DOCUMENT A TYPICAL DAY WHETHER AT HOME OR AWAY. WHEN DID YOU GET UP OR ON THE ROAD? HOW MUCH MONEY DID YOU SPEND ON OUTINGS OR OUT TO LUNCH? WHO DID YOU TRAVEL OR CARPOOL WITH? HOW FAR DID YOU GO OR HOW LONG DID YOU COMMUTE? WHAT WERE YOUR HIGHS AND LOWS? DO YOU HAVE A TRAVEL PATTERN OR DAILY ROUTINE? TYPICAL, IN ANY SITUATION, DOESN'T EVER HAVE TO BE BORING!

Did you KNOW?

RECORD A FUN FACT ABOUT EVERY PERSON YOU MEET THIS WEEK.
JOT DOWN YOUR FINEST & YOUR FUNNIEST THOUGHTS.
(Enter your meeting date, time, and location with each.)

PERSON:

Fun Fact:

DATE/TIME/LOCATION:

PERSON:

Fun Fact:

DATE/TIME/LOCATION:

PERSON:

Fun Fact:

DATE/TIME/LOCATION:

PERSON:

Fun Fact:

DATE/TIME/LOCATION:

PERSON:

Fun Fact:

DATE/TIME/LOCATION:

PERSON:

Fun Fact:

DATE/TIME/LOCATION:

OH THE *Humanity*

DO SOME PEOPLE WATCHING. ALLOW YOUR INNER SOCIOLOGIST TO RUN LOOSE.
PICK SIX PEOPLE OUT OF THE CROWD, THE PASSERSBY, OR THE MIGHTY BUNCH
& TAKE SOME NOTES! *(Favorite people-watching places to get you thinking: the
airport, a café, a park, on a train, or in a plaza in the middle of the city.)*

○ HIPSTER ARTIST
○ BUSINESS TYCOON
○ EAGER YOUNGSTER
○ BEWILDERED TOURIST
○ _____

AGE :

WHAT ARE THEY THINKING?

_____
_____
_____
_____

WHERE ARE THEY GOING?

_____
_____
_____

**WHAT KIND OF SECRET
DO THEY HAVE?**

_____
_____
_____
_____
_____
_____

○ PRIMA BALLERINA
○ HIGH-POWERED EXEC
○ TINY TOT
○ EXPERIENCED TRAVELER
○ _____

AGE :

WHAT ARE THEY THINKING?

_____
_____
_____
_____

WHERE ARE THEY GOING?

_____
_____
_____

**WHAT KIND OF SECRET
DO THEY HAVE?**

_____
_____
_____
_____
_____
_____

○ FASHIONISTA   ○ MEDIA MOGUL

○ CAT LADY   ○ MARATHON RUNNER

○ GRANDE DAME   ○ SCRAPPY STUDENT

○ DOGWALKER   ○ NEW PARENT

○ _____   ○ _____

AGE: AGE:

WHAT ARE THEY THINKING?   **WHAT ARE THEY THINKING?**

WHERE ARE THEY GOING?   **WHERE ARE THEY GOING?**

**WHAT KIND OF SECRET
DO THEY HAVE?**   **WHAT KIND OF SECRET
DO THEY HAVE?**

○ STREET PERFORMER

○ WEEKEND WARRIOR

○ TEENIE BOPPER

○ DEDICATED YOGI

○ _____

AGE :

WHAT ARE THEY THINKING?

_____

_____

_____

_____

WHERE ARE THEY GOING?

_____

_____

_____

**WHAT KIND OF SECRET
DO THEY HAVE?**

_____

_____

_____

_____

_____

_____

_____

_____

_____

_____

_____

○ TECH-SAVVY PROGRAMMER

○ START-UP ENTREPRENEUR

○ WISE OWL

○ STARRY-EYED INGÉNUE

○ _____

AGE :

WHAT ARE THEY THINKING?

_____

_____

_____

_____

WHERE ARE THEY GOING?

_____

_____

_____

**WHAT KIND OF SECRET
DO THEY HAVE?**

_____

_____

_____

_____

_____

_____

_____

_____

_____

_____

_____

Listen IN

SPEND SOME QUALITY TIME EAVESDROPPING & WRITE DOWN BITS
OF OVERHEARD CONVERSATIONS. (Finish their stories, use your creative wit!)

End OF THE LINE

TAKE PUBLIC TRANSPORTATION ALL THE WAY FROM ONE END OF
THE LINE TO THE OTHER. SEE WHAT YOU SEE, TAKE PHOTOS,
GET OFF & BACK ON AGAIN, MAKE NOTES.

DRAW A MAP OF THE ROUTE & GIVE EACH STOP A NAME BASED
ON YOUR INITIAL OBSERVATIONS. *(Feels wild, right?!)*

MY COLLECTION

· ·

OVER THE COURSE OF A WEEK, SET A GOAL TO COLLECT, AMASS, STOCKPILE, HEAP,
OR HOARD ALL THINGS THAT MAKE YOU FEEL LIKE AN EXTREME INVESTIGATOR!
(MAYBE A CLUE, A MAGNIFYING GLASS, YOUR NUMBER TWO PENCILS, OR YOUR BEST
SPECTACLES.) DRAW, IDENTIFY, OR RECORD THEM HERE.

ITEM ....
Date:
....

ITEM ....
Date:
....

ITEM ....
Date:
....

ITEM ....
Date:
....

ITEM ....
Date:
....

ITEM ....
Date:
....

ITEM ....
Date:
....

ITEM ....
Date:
....

SPECIFIC

THINGS TO *Remember:*

A

Chapter of

AUTHENTIC

ADVENTURES

AUTHENTIC

ADVENTURES

This CHAPTER WILL ENCOURAGE THE THOUGHTFUL SOUL-SEARCHER, THE MAGNANIMOUS JOURNEYER, AND THE MINDFUL PIONEER. SO WRAP YOUR ARMS AROUND YOUR BOOK & HEED YOUR OWN INNER MUSINGS, FAVOR THE QUIET, BE KEENLY AWARE OF YOUR SENSES, SIZE UP YOUR WORLD SOFTLY, THOROUGHLY ENGAGE YOUR CHARACTER, BE ABSORBED IN YOUR EXPERIENCES, CONSIDER EVERYTHING, GRANT YOURSELF PERMISSION TO BE PENSIVE, GET LOST IN CONTEMPLATION, PONDER WITH INTENTION & LEAVE THOUGHTFULNESS IN YOUR WAKE.

OKAY, *off you go!*

EAT WITH *Intention*

COOK YOURSELF A MEAL OR EVEN EAT OUT, BUT
MAKE IT THE LONGEST MEAL YOU'VE EVER EATEN.
APPRECIATE EVERY BITE, EVERY MORSEL, EVERY
FLAVOR WITH ALL YOUR SENSES.

....

DRAW THE MEAL & LABEL EVERY PORTION IN POETIC DETAIL
& DESCRIBE YOUR EXPERIENCE. IS IT BRILLIANTLY TANGY,
FULL OF SWEET RADIANCE, BOLDLY PUNGENT, OR FOOLISHLY SPICY?

Date: ....

Portrait OF AN ADVENTURER

· ·

DRAW A SELF-PORTRAIT IN SIX DIFFERENT WAYS!
WHAT NEW THINGS DO YOU SEE IN YOURSELF?

AS A SILHOUETTE

Date: _____   LOCATION: ···

ERASED OUT OF BLACK GRAPHITE

Date: _____   LOCATION: ···

AS A KID

Date: _____

LOCATION:
....

WHEN YOU GET OLDER

Date: _____

LOCATION:
....

WITH YOUR NON-DOMINANT HAND

Date: _____   **LOCATION:** ....

AS A SUPERHERO

Date: _____   **LOCATION:** ....

Drawing
ADVENTURE

....

COLOR THEORY

....

IDENTIFY YOUR FAVORITE
COLOR IN EIGHTEEN THINGS.

DRAW THEM IN MINIATURE
SKETCHES ON THIS PAGE.

ITEM ....
Date: _____ /

ITEM ....
Date: _____ /

ITEM ....
Date: _____ /

ITEM ....
Date: _____ /

ITEM ....
Date: _____ /

ITEM ....
Date: _____ /

ITEM ....
Date: _____ /

ITEM ....
Date: _____ /

ITEM ....
Date: _____ /

ITEM ....
Date: _____ /

ITEM ....
Date: _____ /

ITEM ....
Date: _____ /

ITEM ....
Date: _____ /

ITEM ....
Date: _____ /

ITEM ....
Date: _____ /

ITEM ....
Date: _____ /

ITEM ....
Date: _____ /

ITEM ....
Date: _____ /

Self REALIZATION

TAKE A PHOTO OF YOURSELF EVERY DAY FOR SEVEN DAYS.
USE THE SAME FRAMING & THE SAME TIME OF DAY FOR EVERY PHOTO.
WRITE DOWN YOUR DISCOVERIES.

DAY 1:

DAY 2:

DAY 3:

DAY 4:

DAY 5:

DAY 6:

DAY 7:

PHOTO *Adventure*

EMBARK ON A PHOTO SCAVENGER HUNT!

....

RECORD YOUR FINDINGS WITH DATES & LOCATIONS
FOR A REALLY COOL FUTURE ALBUM!

☐ **YOUR SHADOW**
DATE: LOCATION:

Description:
_____
_____

☐ **A CLOUDY DAY**
DATE: LOCATION:

Description:
_____
_____

☐ **A FACELESS SELF-PORTRAIT**
DATE: LOCATION:

Description:
_____
_____

☐ **SOMEONE ALONE**
DATE: LOCATION:

Description:
_____
_____

☐ **A QUESTION MARK**
DATE: LOCATION:

Description:
_____
_____

☐ **A QUIET SPOT**
DATE: LOCATION:

Description:
_____
_____

☐ **AN IMAGINARY FRIEND**
DATE: LOCATION:

Description:
_____
_____

☐ **A BEAUTIFUL SCENE**
DATE: LOCATION:

Description:
_____
_____

☐ **A BRILLIANT QUOTE**
DATE: LOCATION:

Description:
_____
_____

☐ **YOUR REFLECTION**
DATE: LOCATION:

Description:
_____
_____

Photo FINDINGS

WANDER AROUND, TAKE PICTURES & FIND:

☐ **A SMOOTH PEBBLE**
RELOCATE IT TO
ANOTHER ROCK GARDEN

DATE:
....

LOCATION:
....

DETAILS:
....
....
....

☐ **BREAD**
FEED IT TO
THE BIRDS

DATE:
....

LOCATION:
....

DETAILS:
....
....
....

☐ **HEART-SHAPED LEAF**
PRESS IT INTO
YOUR BOOK

DATE:
....

LOCATION:
....

DETAILS:
....
....
....

☐ **LITTER**
THROW IT IN
THE DUST BIN

DATE:
....

LOCATION:
....

DETAILS:
....
....
....

☐ **YOUR REFLECTION**
TAKE A SELFIE IN
SOMETHING INTERESTING

DATE:
....

LOCATION:
....

DETAILS:
....
....
....

☐ **THE SUNRISE**
ENJOY THE
SOLITUDE

DATE:
....

LOCATION:
....

DETAILS:
....
....
....

☐ **SOMEONE OLDER**
ASK THEM TO TELL
YOU A STORY

DATE:
....

LOCATION:
....

DETAILS:
....
....
....

☐ **A STRANGER**
AT A GROCERY STORE
OFFER TO CARRY THEIR
GROCERIES

DATE:
....

LOCATION:
....

DETAILS:
....
....
....

☐ **A SWING**
PLAY A LITTLE

DATE:
....

LOCATION:
....

DETAILS:
....
....
....

ENTIRELY UP TO *You*

· ·

TODAY, CREATE AN ITINERARY FOR YOURSELF THAT'S ONE HUNDRED PERCENT
AUTHENTIC TO YOU. BE A LITTLE SELFISH. IF YOU'RE ALWAYS WISHING TO LUXURIATE
IN BED UNTIL NOON, DO IT. IF YOUR FAVORITE BREAKFAST IS PANCAKES WITH REAL
BUTTER, CARAMEL SYRUP & CONFETTI SPRINKLES, EAT IT. IF YOU'RE EAGER TO
TAKE A NAP UNDER A TREE, FIND THE TIME. TODAY IS ALL YOURS.

My itinerary:

_____

_____

_____

_____

_____

_____

_____

_____

_____

_____

_____

_____

_____

_____

_____

_____

_____

_____

_____

_____

_____

_____

_____

Date: _____

25 THINGS I'VE DISCOVERED
WHILE *Soul-searching:*

1. _____

2. _____

3. _____

4. _____

5. _____

6. _____

7. _____

8. _____

9. _____

10. _____

11. _____

12. _____

13. _____

14. _____
    _____

15. _____
    _____

16. _____
    _____

17. _____
    _____

18. _____
    _____

19. _____
    _____

20. _____
    _____

21. _____
    _____

22. _____
    _____

23. _____
    _____

24. _____
    _____

25. _____
    _____
    _____

why
I MUST

REFLECT

- ○ TO EXPERIENCE IT ALL FOR THE FIRST TIME
- ○ TO REMAIN MINDFUL
- ○ TO GET OUT OF MY OWN HEAD
- ○ TO GROW WILDLY
- ○ TO LET GO A LITTLE
- ○ TO DESIGN MY OWN LIFE
- ○ TO COLLECT MOMENTS
- ○ TO BE A FREE SPIRIT
- ○ FOR TRAVELING LIGHT
- ○ TO STAY THOUGHTFUL
- ○ TO SIZE UP MY WORLD
- ○ TO MAGNIFY ALL HUMAN EMOTIONS
- ○ TO LIVE FULLY
- ○ TO BE OPEN
- ○ TO EXPERIENCE EACH MOMENT AS IT COMES
- ○ TO REMAIN KEENLY AWARE
- ○ TO ENJOY THE JOURNEY
- ○ TO EMBRACE THE JOURNEY
- ○ TO AWAKEN SOMETHING, EVERYTHING
- ○ IT'S A FINE DAY TO REFLECT
- ○ IN ORDER TO INVEST IN MYSELF
- ○ TO BE FULLY ALIVE
- ○ TO HAVE A DIFFERENT POINT OF VIEW
- ○ TO FIND MYSELF SPEECHLESS
- ○ SO I'M NEVER DISAPPOINTED
- ○ _____
- ○ _____
- ○ _____
- ○ _____

Date: _____

Friend
ADVENTURE

·····························

TODAY, SWAP IDENTITIES WITH A FRIEND,
PARTNER, OR FAVORITE CHUM AND TRY BEING
EACH OTHER FOR THE DAY. DRESS UP IN EACH
OTHER'S CLOTHES, TRADE PHONES, AND GO OUT
INTO THE WORLD TOGETHER. DIG DEEP AND
MAKE THIS AUTHENTIC. HOW DOES IT FEEL TO
WALK IN THEIR SHOES? (MAYBE LITERALLY!)

_____

_____

_____

_____

_____

_____

_____

_____

_____

_____

_____

_____

_____

Name of swapped identity: .... *Date:* ....

WOULD YOU

RATHER?

(CIRCLE YOUR ANSWER)

PLAY IT SOLO *or* STAND IN A CROWD?

WRITE IT DOWN *or* DOODLE ALL OVER?

HAVE AN IMAGINARY FRIEND
or MAKE FIFTY REAL FRIENDS?

CHAT WITH A STRANGER
or GO UNNOTICED?

MEDITATE IN THE MORNING
or SKIP THROUGH THE STREETS?

ENJOY THE SUN RISING *or* BE A STARGAZER?

WALK BAREFOOT *or*
TRAIPSE ABOUT IN YOUR BRIGHT AND SHINYS?

HAVE A NICE DINNER OUT BY YOURSELF
or INVITE THE CREW?

READ *or* WATCH?

CHEW FIFTY TIMES *or*
BITE OFF MORE THAN YOU CAN CHEW?

SHOW YOUR EMOTIONS *or* HOLD THINGS CLOSE?

TAKE A MIDDAY NAP *or* STAY UP ALL NIGHT?

WHISTLE *or* SING?

MAKE A
CHANGE

NOW, MAKE A SWAP OF **WHAT YOU'D RATHER.** TRY OUT THE THINGS
YOU DIDN'T CIRCLE AND CLOSELY OBSERVE YOUR CHANGES! IT'S
GOING TO TAKE GUTS, BUT TACKLING *new things* NEVER HURT ANYONE!

CAN YOU
Keep a Secret?

·························

TODAY EMBARK ON AN INNER ADVENTURE BY
CREATING A LIST OF SPECIAL SECRETS, LITTLE
KNOWN FACTS & INNERMOST THOUGHTS
(THEN FOLD THE PAGE IN HALF AND CARRY ON):

SOMETHING YOU DREAD, SOMEONE YOU LOVE, WHAT
YOU'D RATHER BE DOING, A LITTLE WHITE LIE,
YOUR MOST FREQUENT THOUGHT, WHAT YOU BELIEVE,
A DAYDREAM, WHAT YOU'D LOVE TO DO IN A CROWDED
ELEVATOR, THE PERSON WHO KNOWS YOU BEST, AN ACT
THAT TERRIFIES YOU, YOUR BIGGEST LOSS, SOMETHING
YOU BATTLE, WHO YOU WISH YOU WERE, YOUR BIGGEST
PHOBIA, A MISSED CONNECTION, A BAD HABIT, A BURDEN,
HOW YOU FEEL ABOUT YOURSELF, AN EMBARRASSING LIFE
GOAL, SOMEONE WHO MAKES YOU HAPPY, A CHILDHOOD
JOY, WHAT YOU WANTED TO BE WHEN YOU GREW UP,
WHAT YOU'RE MOST PROUD OF, SOMETHING YOU'RE
THINKING, SOMETHING YOU DO EVERY DAY, YOUR WORST
NIGHTMARE, YOUR BIGGEST PET PEEVE, YOUR FAVORITE
GUILTY PLEASURE, A CRUSH, THE BEST PART OF YOU,
OR SOMETHING YOU'VE NEVER SHARED BEFORE.

Date: _____

Foot THE BILL

. . . .

WHILE YOU'RE OUT TODAY, FIND A WAY TO PAY FOR SOMEONE ELSE IN LINE.
IT MIGHT CHANGE YOUR DAY & IT WILL DEFINITELY CHANGE THEIRS!

Details:

_____

_____

_____

_____

_____

_____

_____

_____

_____

_____

_____

_____

_____

_____

_____

_____

_____

_____

_____

_____

_____

_____

_____

Date: _____

HAPPINESS IS...

Date: ....

GRATITUDE

Date:

SILENCE IS
GOLDEN

GO THROUGH AN ENTIRE DAY TRYING TO STAY AS QUIET AS POSSIBLE.
ADVENTURE WITH CARE, TREAD LIGHTLY, WHISPER ONLY IF YOU HAVE TO.
DOES IT CHANGE HOW YOU APPROACH YOUR WORLD, OTHERS, YOUR DAY?

What things replaced your noise?

Date: _____

Hug
IT OUT

······························

MAKE TODAY *"Free Hug Day,"* PULL YOURSELF UP BY

THE BOOTSTRAPS & PREPARE YOURSELF TO MEET

NEW CHUMS, GIVE FOLKS SOMETHING TO SMILE

ABOUT & A RIGHT STORY TO TELL. CREATE A SIGN

STATING YOUR INTENTION ("FREE HUGS" WOULD BE A

FINE START) AND GO OUT & BE SEEN (& HUGGED)!

BE SURE TO KEEP A TALLY OF YOUR HUGS & WRITE

ABOUT YOUR ENGAGING EXPERIENCE!

_____

_____

_____

_____

_____

_____

_____

_____

_____

_____

_____

Hugs Given: [   ]   *Date:* ·····························

MY COLLECTION

OVER THE COURSE OF A WEEK, SET A GOAL TO COLLECT, AMASS, STOCKPILE, HEAP,
OR HOARD ALL THINGS THAT MAKE YOU FEEL LIKE A MAGNANIMOUS SOUL-SEARCHER!
(MAYBE A TELESCOPE, A MAGIC WAND, YOUR SELF-PORTRAIT, OR A FOUR LEAF
CLOVER.) DRAW, IDENTIFY, OR RECORD THEM HERE.

ITEM ....
Date:
....

ITEM ....
Date:
....

ITEM ....
Date:
....

ITEM ....
Date:
....

ITEM ....
Date:
....

ITEM ....
Date:
....

ITEM ....
Date:
....

ITEM ....
Date:
....

MINDFUL

THINGS TO *Remember:*

A

Chapter of

DARING

ADVENTURES

DARING
ADVENTURES

This CHAPTER FAVORS THE BOLD EXPLORER,

THE GUTSY PIONEER & THE HIGHLY

AUDACIOUS SEEKER. SO TAKE A FIRM HOLD

OF YOUR BOOK & GO FOR BROKE,

PUT ON YOUR CAPE AND SHOW UP UNAFRAID,

PUSH YOUR OWN LIMITS, BE A SMIDGEN

FOOLHARDY, NUDGE YOUR COMFORT ZONE,

TRY NEVER TO BE FAINT OF HEART,

USE YOUR GUTS, PASS AS AN EXTROVERT,

TAKE ON THE WORLD WITH A CHEEKY

GRIN, SQUASH YOUR FEARS & STAND ON

THE EDGE OF THIS ONE BIG ADVENTURE.

NOW, *soldier on!*

Drawing
ADVENTURE

....

NIGHT VISION

....

GO OUTSIDE TONIGHT &
DRAW A SERIES OF SKETCHES
IN THE DARK!

BE BRAVE, TRUST YOUR HAND
& SEE WHAT HAPPENS!
DRAW STANDING UNDER THE
STARS, OUT IN THE DIMNESS
OF A NEIGHBORHOOD
STREET, OR WHILE CLOSING
YOUR EYES COMPLETELY!

Ready, set, go!

ITEM ....
Date:
_____

ITEM ....
Date:
_____

ITEM ....
Date:
_____

ITEM ....
Date:
_____

ITEM ....
Date:
_____

ITEM ....
Date:
_____

ITEM ....
Date:
_____

ITEM ....
Date:
_____

ITEM ....
Date:
_____

ITEM ....
Date:
_____

Draw
ADVENTUROUS
DETAILS

GO & SEE:

SOMETHING HARD TO REACH

Date: Location:

SOMETHING PREPOSTEROUS

Date: / Location:

SOMETHING OUT OF THE ORDINARY

Date: / Location:

SOMETHING ANNOYING

Date: Location:

SOMETHING SCARY

Date: Location:

SOMETHING THAT TROUBLES YOU

Date: / Location:

SOMETHING WACKY

Date: / Location:

SOMETHING OUT OF PLACE

Date: _____ / Location: ....

SOMETHING DISGUSTING

Date: _____ / Location: ....

SOMETHING INSPIRING

Date: / Location:

SOMETHING WILD

Date: / Location:

PHOTO *Adventure*

EMBARK ON A PHOTO SCAVENGER HUNT!

RECORD YOUR FINDINGS WITH DATES & LOCATIONS
FOR A REALLY COOL FUTURE ALBUM!

☐ **A FEAR**
DATE: LOCATION:
Description:
_____
_____

☐ **A SHADOW**
DATE: LOCATION:
Description:
_____
_____

☐ **AN AIRPLANE**
DATE: LOCATION:
Description:
_____
_____

☐ **AN EDGE**
DATE: LOCATION:
Description:
_____
_____

☐ **SOME SORT OF WILDLIFE**
DATE: LOCATION:
Description:
_____
_____

☐ **A CROWD**
DATE: LOCATION:
Description:
_____
_____

☐ **SOMETHING DEEP**
DATE: LOCATION:
Description:
_____
_____

☐ **AN EXCLAMATION MARK**
DATE: LOCATION:
Description:
_____
_____

☐ **A SLOPE**
DATE: LOCATION:
Description:
_____
_____

☐ **SOMETHING HONEST**
DATE: LOCATION:
Description:
_____
_____

☐ **THE MOON**

DATE: LOCATION:

Description:

_____
_____

☐ **FROM A BIRD'S-EYE VIEW**

DATE: LOCATION:

Description:

_____
_____

☐ **SOMETHING ALONE**

DATE: LOCATION:

Description:

_____
_____

☐ **THE TALLEST THING**

DATE: LOCATION:

Description:

_____
_____

☐ **SOMETHING FORGOTTEN**

DATE: LOCATION:

Description:

_____
_____

☐ **THE DARKNESS**

DATE: LOCATION:

Description:

_____
_____

☐ **SOMETHING GIANT**

DATE: LOCATION:

Description:

_____
_____

☐ **FIRE**

DATE: LOCATION:

Description:

_____
_____

☐ **A WARNING SIGN**

DATE: LOCATION:

Description:

_____
_____

☐ **SOMETHING TO CLIMB**

DATE: LOCATION:

Description:

_____
_____

☐ **SOMETHING ESPECIALLY UNUSUAL**

DATE: LOCATION:

Description:

_____
_____

☐ **SOMETHING WITH YOUR EYES CLOSED**

DATE: LOCATION:

Description:

_____
_____

EXOTIC *Tastes*

EXPLORE A GROCERY STORE, A FARMER'S MARKET, OR A MOM-AND-POP CONVENIENT STORE.

PICK UP SIX THINGS YOU'VE NEVER TRIED TO TAKE HOME AND SAMPLE. EATING CAN ALWAYS BE AN ADVENTURE! DRAW & RATE THE DELICIOUSNESS THAT ENSUES.

FOOD:

DATE:

Description:

( ) I COULD EAT THIS EVERY DAY!
( ) IT'S AN ACQUIRED TASTE.
( ) NEVER AGAIN!

FOOD:

DATE:

Description:

( ) I COULD EAT THIS EVERY DAY!
( ) IT'S AN ACQUIRED TASTE.
( ) NEVER AGAIN!

FOOD:

DATE:

Description:

( ) I COULD EAT THIS EVERY DAY
( ) IT'S AN ACQUIRED TASTE.
( ) NEVER AGAIN!

FOOD:

DATE:

Description:

( ) I COULD EAT THIS EVERY DAY!
( ) IT'S AN ACQUIRED TASTE.
( ) NEVER AGAIN!

FOOD:

DATE:

Description:

( ) I COULD EAT THIS EVERY DAY!
( ) IT'S AN ACQUIRED TASTE.
( ) NEVER AGAIN!

FOOD:

DATE:

Description:

( ) I COULD EAT THIS EVERY DAY
( ) IT'S AN ACQUIRED TASTE.
( ) NEVER AGAIN!

MY Hero

PUT ON A CAPE & BRAVE THE DAY!
TAKE PHOTOGRAPHS OF YOURSELF "SAVING" SIX
OTHER PEOPLE FROM HARROWING, PERILOUS,
DISTRESSING, RISKY, DELICATE, ALARMING, OR
FORMIDABLE SITUATIONS. IT'S OBVIOUS THAT
YOU'LL HAVE TO GET CREATIVE, SO WHAT ARE
YOU WAITING FOR, **TIME TO SAVE THE DAY!**

DATE: LOCATION:

Description:

_____

_____

DATE: LOCATION:

Description:

_____

_____

DATE: LOCATION:

Description:

_____

_____

DATE: LOCATION:

Description:

_____

_____

DATE: LOCATION:

Description:

_____

_____

DATE: LOCATION:

Description:

_____

_____

Stand OUTS

TAKE PHOTOGRAPHS OF EIGHT DIFFERENT STRANGERS, DRIFTERS, MAVERICKS,
CHARACTERS & THE OCCASIONAL RARE BIRD. WHAT MAKES EACH SO TOTALLY
UNIQUE? MAYBE IT'S THEIR SHOES? WHAT THEY'RE CARRYING AROUND WITH
THEM? THEIR HAIR COLOR? THEIR CONFIDENT STRIDE? NOW'S YOUR TIME TO
BE BRAVE, TO USE YOUR GUTS. *Go and ask them their name!*

NAME ....

DATE:

LOCATION:

OBSERVATIONS:

_____

_____

_____

_____

_____

_____

_____

_____

_____

_____

_____

_____

_____

_____

_____

NAME ....

DATE:

LOCATION:

OBSERVATIONS:

_____

_____

_____

_____

_____

_____

_____

_____

_____

_____

_____

_____

_____

_____

_____

NAME ....

DATE:

LOCATION:

OBSERVATIONS:

_____

_____

_____

_____

_____

_____

_____

_____

_____

_____

_____

_____

_____

_____

_____

_____

_____

_____

_____

_____

_____

_____

_____

_____

_____

_____

_____

NAME ....

DATE:

LOCATION:

OBSERVATIONS:

_____

_____

_____

_____

_____

_____

_____

_____

_____

_____

_____

_____

_____

_____

_____

_____

_____

_____

_____

_____

_____

_____

_____

_____

_____

_____

_____

NAME ....

DATE:

LOCATION:

OBSERVATIONS:

_____

_____

_____

_____

_____

_____

_____

_____

_____

_____

_____

_____

_____

_____

_____

_____

_____

_____

_____

_____

_____

_____

_____

_____

_____

_____

_____

NAME ....

DATE:

LOCATION:

OBSERVATIONS:

_____

_____

_____

_____

_____

_____

_____

_____

_____

_____

_____

_____

_____

_____

_____

_____

_____

_____

_____

_____

_____

_____

_____

_____

_____

_____

_____

NAME ....

DATE:

LOCATION:

OBSERVATIONS:

_____

_____

_____

_____

_____

_____

_____

_____

_____

_____

_____

_____

_____

_____

_____

_____

_____

_____

_____

_____

_____

_____

_____

_____

_____

_____

NAME ....

DATE:

LOCATION:

OBSERVATIONS:

_____

_____

_____

_____

_____

_____

_____

_____

_____

_____

_____

_____

_____

_____

_____

_____

_____

_____

_____

_____

_____

_____

_____

_____

_____

_____

25 THINGS I'VE DISCOVERE
WHILE *Adventuring:*

1. _____

2. _____

3. _____

4. _____

5. _____

6. _____

7. _____

8. _____

9. _____

10. _____

11. _____

12. _____

13. _____

14. _____

_____

15. _____

_____

16. _____

_____

17. _____

_____

18. _____

_____

19. _____

_____

20. _____

_____

21. _____

_____

22. _____

_____

23. _____

_____

24. _____

_____

25. _____

_____

_____

why
I MUST BE

GUTSY

Just
CHECK
ALL
THAT
APPLY.

○ IN ORDER TO SAY, "HERE GOES NOTHING!"
○ BECAUSE IT'S A WILD RIDE
○ TO BE CONVINCINGLY INTIMIDATING
○ TO DO SOMETHING DIFFERENT
○ TO BUILD UP MY SUPERPOWERS
○ BECAUSE I'M A DAREDEVIL AT HEART
○ TO BE FEARLESS IN THE PURSUIT
○ TO FIND MY SPUNK
○ OUT OF SHEER DETERMINATION
○ SO I REMAIN UNDEFEATED
○ IN ORDER TO BE AMAZING
○ TO LIVE WILDLY
○ TO LIVE A LITTLE ON THE EDGE
○ TO BE FIERCE
○ TO FACE IT ALL WITH SPIRIT
○ TO FEEL ALIVE
○ TO KEEP THINGS UNTAMED
○ BECAUSE NOTHING IS IMPOSSIBLE
○ TO EXPERIENCE SOMETHING WITH PASSION
○ TO FEEL THINGS I'VE NEVER FELT BEFORE
○ TO FEEL EVER SO SLIGHTLY POWERFUL
○ IT'S A FINE DAY FOR AN ADVENTURE
○ TO DISRUPT MY ROUTINE
○ THE WORLD IS WAITING
○ TO FEEL A LITTLE BIT STARTLED
○ BECAUSE THERE ARE NO RULES
○ _____
○ _____
○ _____

Date: _____

Friend
ADVENTURE

....

LIBERATE YOUR VERY BEST FRIEND,

CLOSEST RELATIVE, YOUR FOLKS, THE LITTLES,

THE NEXT OF KIN, OR YOUR COMRADE IN ARMS

FROM THEIR DAILY GRIND, OR MAKE A NEW

FRIEND AND RUN OFF WITH THEM FOR THE DAY.

TODAY IS THE DAY TO TAKE THEM OUT FOR

A MARVELOUS ADVENTURE! SET OFF TO SEE

WHERE THE WIND TAKES YOU!

Date: ....

SAY YES TO
EVERYTHING

WOULD YOU LIKE TO SUPERSIZE THAT? WOULD YOU
LIKE TO TRY IT ON? WOULD YOU LIKE TO HANG OUT
FOR A WHILE? WOULD YOU LIKE ANOTHER?

••••••••••••••••••••••••••

Just. Say. Yes. MAKE A LIST OF EVERYTHING YOU
SAID YES TO TODAY, HOW DID IT FEEL? ARE YOU AS
ADVENTUROUS AS YOU'VE ALWAYS SUPPOSED?

Free RIDE

FIND FREE THINGS TO DO TODAY. YES, ALL DAY! TAKE A HIKE, POP INTO A LOCAL GALLERY, FIND A MUSEUM WITH COMPLIMENTARY ADMISSION, OR HAVE A PICNIC IN THE PARK. MAKE A LIST. THESE MIGHT BE OUT OF THE REALM OF A NORMAL DAY FOR YOU OR THINGS YOU MAY HAVE NEVER THOUGHT TO DO OR HAVE NEVER DONE BEFORE & YOU'LL UNDOUBTEDLY REMARK ON THIS AS A DOWNRIGHT AMAZING ACCOMPLISHMENT!

Date: _____

DRESS
The Part

Today:

- [ ] WEAR A PAPER CROWN
- [ ] A HOMEMADE SUPERHERO CAPE
- [ ] A BRIGHT PINK TUTU
- [ ] A FLASHY FEATHER BOA
- [ ] AN ANIMAL-SHAPED HAT
- [ ] A SIZABLE WIG
- [ ] A COOL PAIR OF SKIING GOGGLES
- [ ] A TOP HAT
- [ ] _____
- [ ] _____

Now, TAKE A CASUAL WALK THROUGH THE NEIGHBORHOOD, SOME CITY STREETS, OR ALL AROUND A STORE. DO YOU FEEL BRAVE? ARE PEOPLE STARING, DOING A BIT OF SNICKERING, ADMIRING YOUR AUDACITY? ENJOY YOUR LATEST COURAGEOUS SPUNK! REMEMBER TO WRITE ABOUT YOUR CHOSEN ADORNMENT BELOW!

. . . .
. . . .
. . . .
. . . .
. . . .
. . . .
. . . .
. . . .
. . . .

Date: _____

BREAK YOUR *Rules*

START BY LISTING THE THINGS YOU DO ALWAYS.

....
....
....
....
....
....
....
....
....
....
....
....
....
....
....
....
....
....
....
....
....
....
....
....
....
....
....

Date: _____

NOW, LIST ALL THE WAYS YOU CAN DO THE OPPOSITE.

Hints: BREAKFAST FOR DINNER, CHIPS INSTEAD OF FRIES, COLORFUL RATHER THAN NEUTRAL, HOT CHOCOLATE TO REPLACE YOUR COFFEE, READ A BOOK AND SKIP THE MOVIE, BROCCOLI AS DESSERT . . .

....
....
....
....
....
....
....
....
....
....
....
....
....
....
....
....
....
....
....
....
....
....
....
....

Date: _____

CAST
A Spell

....

Today, CARRY AROUND A MAGIC WAND. STRIKE UP A
CONVERSATION WITH THREE STRANGERS BY OFFERING, EXTENDING,
DOLING OUT, GRANTING, OR BESTOWING UPON EACH OF THEM
THREE WISHES. ABSOLUTELY KEEP A RECORD OF SAID WISHES!

1.

2.

3.

Date: _____

SAY
Something Nice
· ·

This week, COMPLIMENT STRANGERS.
(EVEN STRANGERS LIKE COMPLIMENTS!)

Date:

GOOF AROUND

LET YOUR FREAK FLAG FLY! GO THROUGH THE DAY DOING SOMETHING RIDICULOUS, ZANY, PREPOSTEROUS, OR COMPLETELY OFFBEAT. HOW DOES IT FEEL?

....

....

....

....

....

....

....

....

....

....

....

....

....

....

....

....

....

....

....

....

....

....

....

....

Date: _____

SOME
perfectly legal
EXAMPLES
MIGHT BE:

NARRATING
EVERYTHING YOU
DO OUT LOUD

SKIPPING EVERY-
WHERE YOU GO

WEARING A
CLOWN NOSE
TO WORK

PRETENDING
YOU'RE A
SUPERHERO

CARRYING A
BALLOON AROUND
WITH YOU

ANNOUNCING
EVERYTHING
YOU'RE THINKING

SCREAMING
"THIS IS BORING!"
EVERY TIME YOU
START TO FEEL
YOUR ATTENTION
WANDERING

Now,
MARCH ALONG!

LIVE
DANGEROUSLY

ACT LIKE YOU'RE INVINCIBLE TODAY!

....

Step on every SIDEWALK CRACK, SPLASH AROUND IN EVERY MUD PUDDLE, CLIMB A TOWERING TREE, STAY IN A FULL BATHTUB UNTIL YOUR FINGERTIPS GET WRINKLY, PET ONLY BLACK CATS, DO CANNONBALLS INTO THE POOL, PARADE RIGHT UNDER THAT LADDER … *I dare you to add thirteen more!*

1. _____

_____

_____

2. _____

_____

_____

3. _____

_____

_____

4. _____

_____

_____

5. _____

_____

_____

6. _____

_____

_____

7. _____

_____

_____

8. _____

_____

_____

9. _____

_____

_____

10. _____

_____

_____

11. _____

_____

_____

12. _____

_____

_____

13. _____

_____

_____

_____

Date: _____

MY COLLECTION

OVER THE COURSE OF A WEEK, SET A GOAL TO COLLECT, AMASS, STOCKPILE, HEAP, OR HOARD ALL THINGS THAT MAKE YOU FEEL LIKE A GUTSY ADVENTURER! (MAYBE A PERMANENT MARKER, A HARD HAT, A SHERIFF'S BADGE, OR YOUR SUPERHERO CAPE.) DRAW, IDENTIFY, OR RECORD THEM HERE.

ITEM ....
Date: ....

ITEM ....
Date: ....

ITEM ....
Date: ....

ITEM ....
Date: ....

ITEM ....
Date: ....

ITEM ....
Date: ....

ITEM ....
Date: ....

ITEM ....
Date: ....

BRAVE

THINGS TO *Remember:*

EPILOGUE

(A SORT OF POST SCRIPT)

GREATEST HITS

(ALSO KNOWN AS RECOMMENDATIONS)

A LIST FOR ALL YOUR FAVORITE PLACES, FOODS,
ADVENTURES, ENCOUNTERS & ADVICE!

WHAT DID YOU BRING HOME?

GROCERIES? SAND IN YOUR SHOES? A BOOK CHOCK-FULL OF
BIG IDEAS? YOUR VERY OWN GRAND ADVENTURE STORY?

THINGS TO
REMEMBER:

WHAT THEY SAID, WHO YOU BUMPED INTO,
WHAT WAS CONQUERED, NEW CHUMS YOU MET.

FUTURE IDEAS:

NEW THINGS TO EXPLORE, ADVENTURES TO REPEAT,
SOMETHING TO SPEND MORE TIME ON.

Brilliantly Adventurous

- MERIT -

BADGES

FEARSOME

Day
DREAMER

I ♥ EXPLORING

Dare TO

-WANDER-

- AWAY -

GO

ADVENTURERS
Club

DREAMING
is
- FREE -

NONCONFORMIST *Society*

Well done. ADVENTURER.

FIELD NOTES,
JOTTINGS
& MUSINGS

FIELD NOTES,
JOTTINGS
& MUSINGS

FIELD NOTES, JOTTINGS
& MUSINGS

FOR MY *Darling Girl,*
THE ADVENTURER
LEADING THE ADVENTURER.

DESIGN & ILLUSTRATIONS BY
Nicole LaRue

....

ISBN: 978-1-4197-2918-8

PUBLISHED IN 2018 BY ABRAMS NOTERIE, AN IMPRINT
OF ABRAMS.

PRINTED AND BOUND IN CHINA

10 9 8 7 6 5 4 3

ABRAMS NOTERIE PRODUCTS ARE AVAILABLE AT
SPECIAL DISCOUNTS WHEN PURCHASED IN QUANTITY
FOR PREMIUMS AND PROMOTIONS AS WELL AS
FUNDRAISING OR EDUCATIONAL USE.

SPECIAL EDITIONS CAN ALSO BE CREATED
TO SPECIFICATION. FOR DETAILS, CONTACT:

SPECIALSALES@ABRAMSBOOKS.COM
OR THE ADDRESS BELOW.

....

ABRAMS The Art of Books
195 Broadway, New York, NY 10007
abramsbooks.com